AMERICA'S ETHNIC DIVERSITY

EUROPEAN AMERICANS

by Moira Rose Donohue

BrightPoint Press

San Diego, CA

BrightPoint Press

an imprint of ReferencePoint Press, Inc.
Printed in the United States

For more information, contact:
BrightPoint Press
PO Box 27779
San Diego, CA 92198
www.BrightPointPress.com

LIBRARY OF CONGRESS CATALOGING-IN-PUBLICATION DATA

Name: Donohue, Moira Rose, author.
Title: European Americans / by Moira Rose Donohue.
Description: San Diego, CA: ReferencePoint Press, 2026 | Series: America's ethnic diversity | Audience: Grade 7 to 9 | Includes bibliographical references and index.
Identifiers: ISBN: 9781678211004 (hardcover) | ISBN: 9781678211011 (eBook)
The complete Library of Congress record is available at www.loc.gov.

CONTENTS

AT A GLANCE

- The first Europeans to arrive in the United States were explorers. They sailed across the Atlantic Ocean from countries such as England, Spain, and France. Many European explorers set up colonies along the eastern coast of what is now the United States.

- During the 1600s and 1700s, large numbers of Europeans immigrated to the United States. Many were from England or Germany. Some came to the United States seeking religious or political freedom.

- In the 1850s, a huge wave of immigrants came to the United States because of a potato famine in Ireland. In the late 1800s, Italian, Greek, and Polish immigrants flocked to the United States.

- Most European immigrants to the United States were Protestant. Others were Catholic. Some Eastern European immigrants were Jewish.

- European immigrants adopted American ways but also brought their own cultures and traditions with them. These included foods and holidays.

- After the 1920s, European immigration to the United States slowed significantly. But in the 1990s and early 2000s, a wave of Eastern Europeans immigrated to the United States.

- Today, most Americans are descendants of European immigrants. Most are descended from English, German, or Irish immigrants. The next most common ancestors are Italian and Polish.

MARY'S JOURNEY

It was 1851. Many people in Ireland relied on potatoes for food. But 6 years earlier, the crop had failed. Year after year, it failed again. Millions of Irish people were starving because of the **famine**. Those who could afford to left Ireland. They traveled elsewhere. They sought food and work.

Teenager Mary Gibney was from County Cavan, Ireland. Her family had only enough

Between 1845 and 1855, millions of Irish people immigrated to escape the potato famine in Ireland. A memorial in Boston, Massachusetts, honors Irish immigrants who came to the United States.

Shred-it

money for one ticket. Mary would travel to the United States alone.

Mary's mother told her to find her uncle Matty Kelly when she arrived. He would help Mary find a job as a maid. Mary held

Many Irish immigrants sailed to the United States on crowded ships. It was often a long and dangerous journey.

back tears. She was scared to leave home. But she would find work. She would send her family the money she earned. Then they'd be able to join her in the United States.

The journey lasted many weeks. The ship rocked. Passengers were crammed together. Finally, the ship reached New York. The ship sailed closer to the harbor. Passengers crowded the deck.

Mary stepped ashore. Tall buildings loomed around her. People bumped into her. They were speaking different languages. New York was nothing like her village at home.

A horse-drawn cab pulled up. The driver asked where Mary was going. He had an Irish accent. Mary told him she was looking for her uncle. The driver recognized her uncle's name. He knew where he lived. He offered Mary a ride. Luckily, many Irish immigrants lived in the same neighborhood. They knew one another.

DIFFERENT PEOPLE, SIMILAR STORIES

Mary was one of many Irish immigrants who came to the United States during the famine. The Irish were just one group that traveled there in the 1800s. Many others came from different European countries. They left home for a variety of reasons. But their stories were similar to Mary's. These immigrant experiences continue today.

Throughout history, European immigrants have settled in United States. Today, the

European Americans have introduced unique cultures and traditions to the United States, shaping the country.

country is home to diverse ethnic groups. Diversity means having groups of people with different ethnic backgrounds. This includes religion, culture, and race. Diversity brings a mix of unique people together. European Americans have played a huge role in shaping the country.

HISTORY OF EUROPEAN AMERICANS

The first Europeans in the United States were explorers. In the late 1400s, many explorers left their home countries. Some came from Spain and Portugal. Others were from France, Italy, and England. These explorers sailed across the sea. Many looked for trade routes to Asia. Instead, the explorers landed in what is now the United States. They found Indigenous peoples living there.

Pedro Menéndez de Avilés founded Saint Augustine, the oldest permanent European settlement in the United States. Today, a statue of him stands in the city.

Augustine Florida
Home Of
Lightner Museum
DON PEDRO MENENDEZ DE AVILES

FIRST SETTLERS

European countries wanted to claim the newly discovered land. Countries such as Spain and France fought over it. King Phillip II ruled Spain. He sent Pedro Menéndez de Avilés to the United States. The king ordered Menéndez de Avilés to push French explorers off some land. This land was in what is now Florida. Menéndez de Avilés defeated the French. He built a fort in what would become Saint Augustine, Florida.

Menéndez de Avilés thought Spain should send settlers to the land. He wrote to the king. He said, "In these provinces . . . there will be much wine, many sugar mills, a great number of livestock—there are . . . hemp, tar, pitch and lumber, which Your

Majesty does not have in your kingdoms."[1] King Phillip II agreed. In 1565, Saint Augustine became the first permanent European settlement in the United States.

In 1607, English settlers landed in what is now Virginia. Captain Christopher Newport led the group. When they arrived, the settlers opened a box. It contained instructions. They were from King James I

English settlers founded Jamestown in 1607. Today, people can visit the site and learn about the people who once lived there.

The Pilgrims left England because they wanted religious freedom. They settled in Plymouth, Massachusetts, in 1620.

of England. He told the settlers to set up a **colony**. It would be the first permanent English-speaking colony. The settlers named it Jamestown.

COMING TO COLONIAL AMERICA

These early settlers were the first European immigrants to the United States.

Historians are unsure how many Europeans made the journey. Some think around 600,000 Europeans came to the United States between 1600 and 1800. Early settlements there became colonies. By 1763, England had several colonies in the area. People in these colonies were ruled by the British.

Most settlers came voluntarily. Some became indentured servants. These servants worked under a contract. They served a person or household. They were often paid little. Most contracts lasted 4 or 5 years. The servants were free once their contracts ended.

Some Europeans came to the United States for religious freedom. This included the Puritans and the Pilgrims.

These religious groups came from English-speaking countries. Their countries forced citizens to follow certain religions. Others came for political reasons. They wanted to escape their home country's government. They disagreed with their rulers' policies. Many were **persecuted** for their views.

Other European immigrants wanted land. They asked for land grants in the colonies. They claimed the land when they arrived. But Indigenous peoples had been living there for thousands of years. Immigrants and Indigenous peoples fought over the land.

In 1776, the colonies declared their independence from the British king. They fought England in the American

Revolutionary War (1775–1783). They won and set up a new government. The colonies would later become the first US states.

THE POTATO FAMINE

In the mid-1800s, a wave of Irish immigrants arrived in the United States. Most were farmers. In Ireland, they grew crops on

During the potato famine, many Irish people left their homes to find work in the United States.

Steamships made the journey to the United States much shorter, sparking new waves of European immigration to the country.

British-owned land. They sent the crops to English landlords as rent. They grew potatoes to eat. But one year, the potatoes turned black. They had a disease called the blight. The blight lasted for many years.

Without potatoes, many Irish people had no food. More than a million died. Many families needed money. They sent family members to the United States. There, they could find work. Almost 2 million Irish people immigrated to the United States or Australia between 1845 and 1855.

These Irish immigrants were mostly Catholic. Many Protestants in the United States didn't trust them. Businesses posted signs that they were hiring. But the signs said, "No Irish Need Apply."[2]

STEAMBOATS AND SWEATSHOPS

In the 1800s, sailing across the Atlantic Ocean took many weeks. The journey was difficult. Jozef Kostlan was a Czech immigrant. In 1863, he wrote a letter home after sailing to the United States. He said, "[The ship] began to rock us so unpleasantly that we could not fall asleep."[3]

Beginning in 1892, European immigrants coming to the United States were processed at Ellis Island. Many had to wait in long lines and pass health exams.

In 1819, the first steamboat sailed across the Atlantic Ocean. The trip took about 4 weeks. But over time, steamboat engines improved. By the 1880s, the trip took only a week. This sparked a huge wave of immigration. It lasted until 1920. From 1815 to 1915, more than 30 million Europeans arrived in the United States.

Italians, Greeks, and Eastern Europeans came during this time. Some wanted better lives. They hoped to make money in the United States. Many Eastern European immigrants were Jewish. In the 1880s, the Russian government attacked Jewish towns in Eastern Europe. People immigrated to escape these attacks.

Many European immigrants settled in US port cities. Some could find work only in sweatshops, or factories. Working hours were long in sweatshops. Wages were low. Working conditions were unsafe. Immigrants also struggled to find housing. Many lived in crowded apartments.

BARRIERS AND CHALLENGES

In the 1800s, many European immigrants entered the United States through Castle Garden. This is in New York City.

Immigrants were processed there. Soon, the United States needed a bigger facility. In 1892, Ellis Island opened in New York City. Here, government workers recorded immigrants' names as they arrived.

Ellis Island

Many European immigrants were processed at Ellis Island. They waited in lines for medical exams. Euterpe Dukakis was a Greek immigrant. She arrived at Ellis Island in 1913. She later spoke about the medical exams. She said, "We were all frightened that they would not find us completely healthy and turn us back." After the exams, immigrants provided their names. Finally, they were given a meal.

Source: Philip Chrysopoulos, "Ellis Island: The First Sight of America for Thousands of Greeks," Greek Reporter, *April 11, 2025. https://greekreporter.com.*

Many Americans worried about immigration. They thought immigrants were taking their jobs. Some had racist or sexist views about immigrants.

In 1882, the US Congress decided to limit immigration. It passed the Immigration Act of 1882. This made it harder for all immigrants to enter the country. They had to pass health exams. People with contagious diseases were turned away. So were people with mental disorders. A 1917 law also required that immigrants know how to read and write English. In 1924, the government set up **quotas**. These limited the number of immigrants who could settle in the country based on their country of origin.

CHAPTER TWO

CULTURES AND TRADITIONS

Europe is made up of 44 countries. Each country has different cultures. People speak different languages.

In the United States, early European immigrants often tried to find relatives and friends from their country. Many settled in the same areas. Some followed American ways. People thought of the country as a melting pot. They wanted to "melt" into US culture. But many immigrants wanted

Some European Americans celebrate their cultural identities through traditional dance and music.

to keep their traditions too. Over time, European Americans developed unique cultural identities. Today, they continue to celebrate their **heritage**.

ENGLISH SPEAKERS

Most people in Colonial America were of British descent. They spoke English. At the time, England was ruled by a monarch. This monarch ruled the colonies too. The colonists wanted to govern themselves. This is why they fought for independence. But the colonists liked other parts of British government. Colonist Alexander Hamilton said the British government was "the best in the world."[4] The founding fathers liked England's Parliament. Members of Parliament made laws. They acted as representatives of the people. The US founding fathers borrowed this idea.

English immigrants also brought the English language to the United States. Today, many languages are spoken in the country. But all US government documents

The founding fathers borrowed some aspects of British government to create the US government.

In Chicago, Illinois, people celebrate Saint Patrick's Day by dyeing a section of the Chicago River green. The color green is a symbol of Irish culture.

are written in English. Most Americans also speak English.

IRISH TRADITIONS

Irish Americans brought traditions to the United States too. One was storytelling. They told tales of fairies and leprechauns.

Today, many people believe Halloween has Irish origins. Celtic peoples in Ireland celebrated the dead. They did so at the beginning of the winter. This developed into the modern holiday of Halloween.

The Irish also introduced Saint Patrick's Day. It honors the patron saint of Ireland. Patron saints are saints associated with places or things. Irish Americans turned it into a major US holiday. People celebrate Irish culture. They have parties and parades.

Irish Americans have also helped shape US society. Irish immigrants acted to protect workers in the United States. They organized labor unions. One Irish immigrant was Mary Harris Jones, or Mother Jones. She helped establish unions in the late 1800s and early 1900s.

GERMAN SPEAKERS

German-speaking immigrants came to the United States from Germany and Austria. They brought foods to the United States. This includes hot dogs. German Americans introduced holiday traditions. At Christmastime, they decorated trees.

German Americans contributed to the US education system. Margarethe Schurz

Pretzels

The pretzel was first created by European monks. The pretzel's three loops were symbolic. It represented the belief that God was three persons in one. German immigrants brought pretzels to the United States. Pretzels were practical. They were hard. And they lasted longer than bread. Today, pretzels are considered a staple American snack.

The city of Lindstrom, Minnesota, was founded by Swedish immigrants and is now known as "America's Little Sweden."

introduced kindergarten. She opened the first public kindergarten in 1856.

SCANDINAVIANS

Other immigrants to the United States were from Northern Europe. This region is known as Scandinavia. It includes Norway, Sweden, and Denmark. Most Swedish immigrants were farmers. Many settled in midwestern states that had farmland. These included Minnesota and Wisconsin.

Sweden was known for setting up public organizations. Swedish Americans continued this tradition. They opened free schools in the United States. Dr. Nils Johanson was a Swedish immigrant. He built a nonprofit hospital in Seattle, Washington. It was completed in 1910.

ITALIANS

Most Italian immigrants came to the United States in the late 1800s. By 1920, more than 4 million Italians had come to the country. Many sought work.

Italian Americans introduced new foods to the United States, including pasta and pizza.

Italian immigrants introduced people in the United States to many new foods. One was chicken tetrazzini. It is made with pasta. Italian Americans also introduced pizza. Today, this is one of the top ten foods eaten in the United States. In Italy, people often grew grapes. They turned the grapes into wine. Italian immigrants set up wineries on the western US coast.

EASTERN EUROPEANS

During the 1880s and 1890s, Eastern Europeans arrived in the United States. Many were from Poland. Polish Americans introduced holiday traditions. These were for Christian holidays such as Easter. They also cooked special foods. This included pierogi. These are half-moon-shaped dumplings.

Other Eastern Europeans came from Russia and Hungary. They were often Jewish. They set up businesses such as clothing factories. Others worked in banking. Jewish bankers introduced certain types of loans to US banks. These changed American banking practices.

Traditional Polish pierogi are often filled with potatoes, cheese, or meat. The dumplings are sometimes served with sour cream or fried onions.

CHAPTER THREE

RELIGIONS

European Americans have had a big effect on religion in the United States. The earliest European settlers were Spanish. Spain was a Catholic country. Many Spanish settlers spread Catholicism in what is now the United States. But things changed in the early 1600s. By that time, almost all European immigrants to the country were Protestant.

Early Spanish settlers in the United States set up Catholic churches called missions. They worked to convert Indigenous peoples to Christianity.

Like Catholics, Protestants are Christian. They believe in Jesus Christ. But they worship differently. Many Protestant Europeans left their home countries. They weren't allowed to freely practice their religion there. They sought religious freedom in the United States.

PILGRIMS AND PURITANS

The Pilgrims were an English religious group. They wanted to separate from the Church of England. This was a Protestant **sect** in England. The Pilgrims moved to the Netherlands. But they faced economic hardships there. So they traveled to the American colonies. They arrived there in 1620. They landed in Plymouth, Massachusetts.

Puritan settlers in the United States followed strict religious laws and lifestyles.

The Puritans were another early Protestant group. They arrived in North America in the mid-1600s. They were also from England. They wanted a simpler form of religion. They had strict views of right and wrong. Their teachings shaped US government systems and ideas of morality. But Puritans wanted everyone to worship as they did. Many did not treat Catholics equally.

Many historic Protestant churches in the United States are still in use today. One of the oldest is Gloria Dei Church in Philadelphia, Pennsylvania, which was founded by Swedish Lutherans.

Some Protestant immigrants disagreed with this approach. The Quakers settled in Pennsylvania. This group encouraged religious **tolerance**. Roger Williams was a minister. He founded Rhode Island in 1636. He believed in the separation of church and state. He said, "God requireth not [a] uniformity of Religion to be [enacted] and [enforced] in any civil state."[5]

OTHER CHRISTIAN GROUPS

Other Protestant groups came to the United States too. These included Lutherans and Baptists. In the 1850s, Danish immigrants settled in the midwestern United States. They spread a new religion that grew from Protestantism. It was called Mormonism. Over time, these groups influenced religious traditions in the United States. They broke into sects. Today, 71 percent of white Americans say they are Christian. Half of those identify as Protestant.

Protestants and Catholics introduced several religious holidays. One is Christmas. It celebrates the birth of Jesus.

Another major holiday is Easter. It celebrates Jesus's resurrection. Unlike Protestants, Catholics also celebrate holidays associated with Christian saints.

JUDAISM

In the 1880s, many European Jews immigrated to the United States. They were mostly from Eastern Europe. They came to

Santa Claus

Dutch immigrants introduced a popular Christmas tradition. They shared the story of Saint Nicholas, or Sinterklaas. He was a bishop. He gave presents to children. The Dutch honor this figure on December 6. This is Saint Nicholas's feast day. People exchange gifts. English settlers combined this tradition with their story of Father Christmas. The result was Santa Claus.

escape anti-Jewish movements. Between 1933 and 1945, the Nazis persecuted European Jews during the Holocaust. Six million Jews were murdered. Many were killed at concentration camps in Europe. Waves of Jews fled to the United States during this time. Many came after the war too. In 2020, about 5.8 million US adults identified as Jewish.

Jews have a Sabbath. This day of prayer and rest happens every Saturday. Jewish people do not believe Jesus was the Son of God.

Jewish people celebrate different holidays than Christians. One is Rosh Hashanah, the Jewish New Year. Another is Hanukkah, a festival of lights.

CHAPTER FOUR

EUROPEAN AMERICANS TODAY

Since the 1960s, European immigration to the United States has declined. Most immigrants come from other continents. Today, only 10 percent of all immigrants to the United States are European.

However, most white people in the United States are **descendants** of European immigrants. In 2020, white Americans were asked about their heritage. More than half said they had **ancestors** who were English,

In 2020, 45 million white Americans reported having German heritage.

GTV

Actress Helen Mirren was born in England but became a US citizen in 2017.

German, or Irish immigrants. The next most common ancestors were Italian and Polish.

THE ENGLISH

Some early English immigrants were given land in Virginia. They settled there. Workers from England often settled in the New England region. Today, their descendants are spread out evenly across the United States.

About 20,000 British people move to the United States each year. Most go to New York City. Others find homes in Boston, Massachusetts; Los Angeles, California; or Austin, Texas. Many British people move for work.

One famous British American is actress Helen Mirren. She became a US citizen in 2017. Talk show host John Oliver is also British American.

THE IRISH

Irish immigrants often settled in Boston and New York. Many Irish girls and women worked as maids. Men worked on railroads.

Over the years, Irish Americans moved into other jobs. Many joined the police force. Most Irish Americans stayed close to the coast. Today, their descendants live mainly in Massachusetts, New Hampshire, and New York.

In 1960, John F. Kennedy became the first Irish Catholic to be elected US president.

Many Americans have Irish heritage. One is animator Walt Disney. Others include actress Grace Kelly and singer Bruce Springsteen. US president John F. Kennedy was Irish Catholic.

GERMANS

Many German-speaking immigrants originally settled in Virginia. Later, they moved to the farmlands of Pennsylvania. German Americans helped build railroads. They settled nearby. That's why most German Americans now live in the Midwest. Some are farmers or skilled workers. Others are intellectuals and scientists. In colonial times, there were often as many Germans in the country as there were English people. That's still true today.

One famous German American was physicist Albert Einstein. He immigrated to the United States in 1932. Other German Americans include author Kurt Vonnegut and pilot Amelia Earhart.

SCANDINAVIANS

Early Scandinavian immigrants settled along the Delaware River. This runs through several states on the East Coast. They set up a large colony near the river. They called it New Sweden.

Swedish Americans soon headed west. A new law passed in 1862. Under it, people could get free land. To do so, they had to farm it for 5 years. Many Swedes and Scandinavians moved to the midwestern United States. There, they claimed farmland.

TOP IMMIGRANT POPULATIONS IN US STATES, 1910

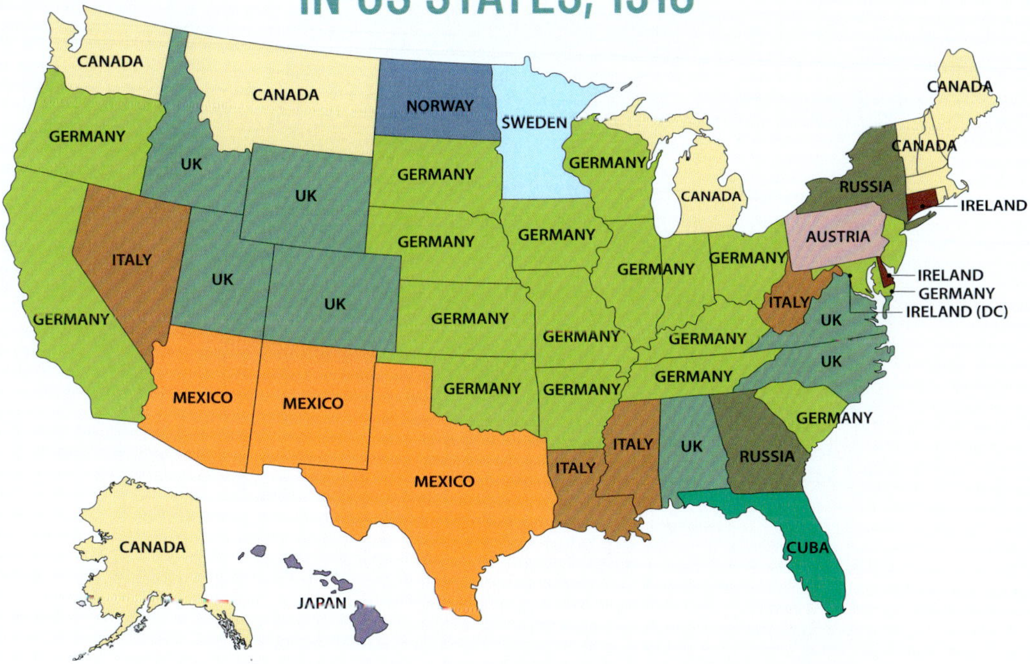

Throughout the 1800s and 1900s, European immigrants settled in different regions of the United States. This map shows the top immigrant populations in each US state in 1910.

Today, their descendants still live in the region. States such as Minnesota, North Dakota, and Wisconsin are cultural centers for Scandinavian Americans.

One notable Scandinavian American was actress Greta Garbo. She was born in Sweden. She immigrated to the

United States in 1925. Astronaut Buzz Aldrin has Swedish heritage too.

ITALIANS

Early Italian immigrants often settled in New York City. They formed their own neighborhood there. They called it Little Italy. Here, they could celebrate Italian feast days. Today, Little Italy is a popular place. Many people go there for authentic Italian food.

Other Italian Americans moved to cities such as Chicago and Baltimore, Maryland. These also have Little Italy neighborhoods. Today, the area with the highest percentage of Italian Americans is in New Jersey.

Singer Frank Sinatra and baseball player Joe DiMaggio were famous

In New York City's Little Italy neighborhood, people can enjoy street fairs and authentic Italian food.

Italian Americans. Singer Lady Gaga and actor Al Pacino also have Italian roots. So does Dr. Anthony Fauci.

EASTERN EUROPEANS

From 1990 to 2000, the number of European immigrants increased. Almost half were Eastern European. This new wave was a result of political changes. The Soviet Union dissolved in 1991. Russia, Ukraine, and other areas of the Soviet Union became separate countries. Czechoslovakia and Yugoslavia split into several other countries. These changes brought many immigrants to the United States.

One notable Eastern European American is gymnast Nastia Liukin. She is from Russia. Filmmaker Steven

Madeleine Albright

As a child, Madeleine Albright immigrated from the Czech Republic. She became a US citizen in 1957. Later, she became the US representative to the United Nations. She also served as the first female secretary of state. In 2012, Albright received the Presidential Medal of Freedom. She said, "My driving force is that I want to make a difference."

Source: Marianne Schnall, "'I Have Had a Remarkable Life': A Tribute to Madeleine Albright," Forbes, *March 24, 2022. www.forbes.com.*

Spielberg and actress Mila Kunis have Ukrainian heritage.

Today, European Americans shape the United States in many ways. They carry on diverse traditions. They continue to be a key part of the American story.

Russian American gymnast Nastia Liukin won a gold medal at the 2008 Olympic Games in Beijing, China.

GLOSSARY

ancestors

family members who lived long ago

colony

an area in a country that is ruled and settled by people from another country

descendants

relatives who come after someone in a family tree

famine

a serious food shortage

heritage

practices and characteristics passed down from one generation to the next

persecuted

treated unfairly because of one's race, ethnicity, or religious beliefs

quotas

limits on the amount of something

sect

a religious group that has split off from a larger religious group

tolerance

willingness to accept beliefs that are different from one's own

SOURCE NOTES

CHAPTER ONE: HISTORY OF EUROPEAN AMERICANS

1. Quoted in "Pedro Menéndez de Avilés, Letter to King Philip II," *Early Visions of Florida*, n.d. https://earlyfloridalit.net.

2. Quoted in Mark Bulik, "1854: No Irish Need Apply," *New York Times*, September 8, 2015. www.nytimes.com.

3. Quoted in Daniel Necas, "Jozef Kostlan, Letter 1863/12/26," *University of Minnesota Immigration History Research Archives*, n.d. https://ihrca.umn.edu/immigrant-letters.

CHAPTER TWO: CULTURES AND TRADITIONS

4. Quoted in "Constitution of the United States—A History," *National Archives*, October 7, 2021. www.archives.gov.

CHAPTER THREE: RELIGIONS

5. Quoted in "Roger Williams, Rhode Island Founder," *Library of Congress*, n.d. www.loc.gov.

FOR FURTHER RESEARCH

BOOKS

Tammy Gagne, *Refugee and Immigrant Rights*. BrightPoint Press, 2025.

Emma Kaiser, *Jewish Americans*. BrightPoint Press, 2026.

Margeaux Weston and Sarosh Arif, *We Are the United States*. Wide Eyed Editions, 2022.

INTERNET SOURCES

"Immigration and Relocation in US History: Irish," *Library of Congress*, n.d. www.loc.gov.

"Immigration to the United States," *Britannica*, n.d. https://kids.britannica.com.

"Overview and History: Ellis Island," *Statue of Liberty–Ellis Island Foundation*, n.d. www.statueofliberty.org.

WEBSITES

Ellis Island

www.statueofliberty.org/ellis-island

Ellis Island is a historic site in New York and New Jersey. It features the National Museum of Immigration. Its website hosts an immigrant arrival archive and information about European immigrants in the United States.

Library of Congress: Immigration and Relocation in US History

www.loc.gov/classroom-materials/immigration

The Library of Congress's Immigration and Relocation in US History collection features information about European immigrants to the United States. The collection highlights people from several European countries, including England, Ireland, Germany, Sweden, and Italy.

National Museum of American History

https://americanhistory.si.edu

The National Museum of American History is part of the Smithsonian in Washington, DC. It features exhibits on US culture and history, including the history of immigration. Its website hosts information about current exhibits, an online gallery of the museum's collections, and educational resources.

INDEX

IMAGE CREDITS

Cover: © Oleksandra Kharkova/iStockphoto
5: © Monkey Business Images/Shutterstock Images
7: © travelview/Shutterstock Images
8: © Everett Collection/Shutterstock Images
11: © Steve Edreff/Shutterstock Images
13: © FL Golden Hour/Shutterstock Images
15: © visionsofmaine/iStockphoto
16: © Artgen/Alamy
19: © Everett Collection/Shutterstock Images
20: © Everett Collection/Shutterstock Images
22: © Everett Collection/Shutterstock Images
27: © Roberto Galan/Shutterstock Images
29: © andipantz/iStockphoto
30: © Tzido Sun/Shutterstock Images
33: © Sam Wagner/Shutterstock Images
35: © Little Vignettes Photo/Shutterstock Images
37: © paulinarz/Shutterstock Images
39: © Nutmegoo7/Shutterstock Images
41: © Artgen/Alamy
42: © Daniel M. Silva/Shutterstock Images
47: © Steve Edreff/Shutterstock Images
48: © Jaguar PS/Shutterstock Images
50: © Cecil Stoughton/National Archives
53: © Red Line Editorial
55: © Apostolis Giontzis/Shutterstock Images
57: © Tony Marshall/PA Images/Alamy

ABOUT THE AUTHOR

Moira Rose Donohue is the author of more than forty nonfiction books for children. Her books have received numerous starred reviews, and she was awarded the Florida Book Award Silver Medal for Young Children's Literature in 2021. Donohue's maternal grandparents immigrated to the United States from Portugal. Her paternal great-grandmother, Mary Gibney, immigrated from Ireland during the potato famine. Originally from New York City, Donohue lives in Florida.